More....
Scout Skits

**A collection of more than
75 favorite campfire skits**

Printed in the United States.
Eighth Printing – National Edition

Scout Fun Books is not officially affiliated with the Boy Scouts of America, Girl Scouts of America or the World Organization of Scouting.

Scout Fun Books
c/o Thomas C. Mercaldo
154 Herbert Street
Milford, CT 06461

How to use this book

Listed at the beginning of each skit are the number of participants required and any props which may be needed. Generally, there is a minimum number needed to perform each skit, however, additional participants can usually be added. The dialog between participants is in plain text, while instructions for actors are listed in italics. Variations, when they exist, follow each skit.

Preface

Due to the great popularity of Scout Skits, I have put together a second collection of campfire skits for use by Scouters. These two books are intended to be used as a set, with this book containing a complete index of the skits found in each edition (*Scout Skits* and *More Scout Skits*).

I sincerely hope that you enjoy these skits, and that this publication is a tool to help you create outstanding campfires.

Tom Mercaldo

4

Table of Contents

The Invisible Bench

Participants: 4 minimum
Props: None

The first participant is squatting as though he were sitting on an invisible bench. A second Camper comes in and begins the dialog.

2nd Camper: What are you doing?
1st Camper: I'm sitting on the invisible bench.
2nd Camper: Can I join you?"
1st Camper: Sure, there's plenty of room.
Second boy pretends to sit. A third boy comes along, and the scene repeats. This can be done with as many boys as there are in the patrol. Finally the last boy comes along and asks,
Last Camper: What are you doing?
1st Camper: I'm sitting on the invisible bench.
Last Camper: But I moved it over there this morning!

AAAAHHHHHH!! All the seated boys fall down.

e Loon Hunt

articipants: 5
Props: None

Narrator: This is the story of the little-known Medicrin and two hunters' efforts to capture it. *The Medicrin, which has been dancing around during the Narrator's speech, suddenly spots the two hunters, who blunderingly, and unsuccessfully, attempt to catch the Medicrin. During the next speech, all actors act according to the Narrator's storyline.*
Narrator: Several times our bold hunters attempted to catch this
Medicrin: they use traps, "Medicrin" calls, even a sick loon. *Every once in a while the actors make appropriate comments.* But all this was to no avail. Finally, they consulted a wise man.
Hunter 1: Wise man, we have been trying to catch the Medicrin for quite a while, but without any success. We even tried to lure it with a sick loon, because we'd heard that it was a good idea. What do you suggest?

Wise man: *Speaks in an old, strained, many years-of-experience, sage voice.* You have been going about it in almost the right way. But the Medicrin also needs a sweeter trap!

Hunter 1: *Bewildered* Uh... Thank you, Wise man! Let's go!

Hunter 2: What did he mean by a sweeter trap?

Hunter 1: I don't know. Maybe we should feed our sick loon some sugar!

Hunter 2: Sugar?

Hunter 1: Yeah! You know, like sugar cured ham!

Narrator: And so our brave hunters took a bag of sugar and forced it down the loon's throat. Ahh ... Watch now as the Medicrin spots our loon.

The Medicrin sees the loon and DIVES for it, at which point, the hunters capture the Medicrin.

Narrator: Our brave hunters have finally succeeded in capturing the Medicrin. Which, just proves that ... A loonful of sugar helps the Medicrin go down!

The Vampire Skit

Participants: 2
Props: None

Scene: One vampire, standing onstage, takes a can marked "blood", pours tomato juice from it into a glass and drinks it. The second vampire enters.

Vampire #1: Mmm. Delicious. Vould you like some?

Vampire #2: No, thanks. I couldn't drink another bite.

Vampire #1: So vat's new?

Vampire #2: Nothing much. I just saw a poor old bum begging on the street corner.

Vampire #1: You did. Vat did he say?

Vampire #2: He vanted me to help him. He said he hadn't had a bite in days.

Vampire #1: So what did you do?

Vampire #2: Vat else? Naturally, I bit him!

Running Deer

Participants: 2
Props: Indian costume (optional)

The skit begins with a young boy addressing an Indian Chief.

Scout: Mighty Chief, why was my brother named Running Deer?
Chief: Because on the day he was born, I saw a dear running past my teepee.
Scout: Why was my sister named Flying Eagle?
Chief: Because on the night she was born I saw a Flying Eagle.
Scout: And why was my older sister named Galloping Buffalo?
Chief: Because on the night that she was born, I saw a Galloping Buffalo. Why do you ask me so many questions, Bear Throwing Up?

Dragon Breath

Participants: 4 to 7
Props: Blanket

A Scout draped in a blanket plays the part of a terrible dragon with terrible breath. Three or four "volunteers" are "planted" at various points in the audience; they are selected to come up one at a time to say hello to the dragon. Each time a Scout says hi to the dragon, the dragon replies, "Hello!" and the "volunteer" falls over dead (there is a lot of room for Scouts to ham this up). Finally, a real volunteer is selected to say hello to the dragon. When he says, "Hello, Dragon," the dragon falls over dead.

Hat and Candle Skit

Participants: 1 or 4
Props: Various hats and a candle

This skit is best performed by one person, although it can be done with 4 performers. A single performer uses various hats and voice intonations to indicate which character is speaking. The Mother talks in a high voice with the lower lip out and up, and wears a fancy shower hat. The Father wears a ball cap with the peak to the left side and talks out of the left side of his mouth. The educated son, speaks in a normal voice, and wears the ball cap to the front. The other son wears the cap to the right, and talks out of that side. The father and other son have drawls. The candle is burning, in front of the performer.

Father:	Well, it is sure good having you home from college son. Hope you're getting a good education.
Ed Son:	Oh I am, it won't be long and I'll graduate.
Son:	Sure enough you won't want to be stayin' down here on the farm.
Mother:	Now, Marvin, Tom'll be visitin' often enough.
Father:	[yawning] It's been a long day, and hearin' about all that college learnin' has made me tired. I'm goin' ta turn in.
All:	[indicate agreement]
Mother:	This durn'd candle's always a problem to put out, but out it's got to go. [tries to blow it out, but because of lip, air goes up] Hey Pa, I can't do it again, you try it
Father:	[blows, but air goes sideways] Cain't do it neither Ma. Marvin, you have a go.
Son:	[blows, and blows, but air goes to other side] Ain't no good Pa. I try and try, but all I get is chapped lips. Tom, show us what all that educamation has done fer ya.
Ed Son:	[licks finger and thumb, pinches out flame - exits]

Gravity Check

Participants: 2
Props: None

Two scouts walk on stage. The first scout stops suddenly and says, "Gravity check!" Both scouts jump, and then the second scout says, "Still working!

The Brain Shop

Participants: 2
Props: None

Customer: (to shopkeeper) Hi! I'm bored with myself. I'd like to buy a new brain and have an all-new personality.

Shopkeeper: (In one of those evil, horror movie voices) Ahh, yes. Well, I can sell you this brain from Billy Crystal for $5000. Hcrc. Try it. ("Unscrews" head and plops in pretend brain.) How do you feel?

Customer: (In Billy Crystal's voice) Marvelous. I ... feel ... marvelous. But I don't think it's me. Can I try another?

Shopkeeper: Okay. Let me see. (Rummages around.) Let's try this one. It's the brain from Captain Kirk. Only $5000.

Customer: (In Kirk voice) Scotty ... Can you fix those transporters? No, a bit too dramatic for me.

Shopkeeper: Sure. I'll go out back. (Rummages around in back of store.) Here's one from President George W. Bush. It only costs $5000. How do you feel?

Customer: (Mispronouncing words) Not sophtimacated enuff for me ... I think I'd like to try another.

Shopkeeper: Hmmmm. A tough customer. I'll have to go down to the basement. I'll be back. (Customer comments on the kind of brains he has gotten and what kind he'll get next.) Ahhh, here we are. The best in the house. I guarantee you'll love it. Only $15000. Yes ... $15000.

Customer: (Imitates a leader in the audience who may be well known for a certain phrase or a certain way of talking.) Hmmm ... this is good. But I recognize it. No, wait ... it's (Insert name of this known Scoutleader) I love it! But tell me ..... the brains of those three famous people only cost $5000 apiece. This one is from a virtually unknown Scoutleader. Why does it cost $15000?

Shopkeeper: Well, it's never been used!

Uncoordinated Actions

Participants: 2
Props: Long sleeve shirt and a sheet or blanket

This skit can be performed in a variety of ways. The central concept of the skit is one person performs some act while another individual who cannot be seen by the audience provides the hand motions for the performer. The performer can be an opera singer, and the hand motions can be done at inappropriate times during the song. These stray hands can cover the singer's mouth or eyes during the performance, or the singer's stomach can be rubbed or his face slapped. There is really no limit to what can be done with this skit. Here's how the skit is done:

A large button down shirt is fastened backwards around the singer/performer. The singer/performer does not place his arms in the shirtsleeves. A second individual (the uncoordinated actor) stands behind the first, placing his arms through the shirtsleeves. A sheet is placed between the singer/uncoordinated performer so that the uncoordinated performer cannot be seen (It is best to cut a sheet specially for this purpose, but this skit will work simply by draping a sheet in a position such that the head of the "uncoordinated performer" is not seen.

Variations: This skit can be performed with more than one set of singers/uncoordinated actors. Another variation involves no singing at all, performers/uncoordinated actors can simply try to perform simple acts in line with the performer's narration like making a sandwich, eating from a bowl, tying shoes, etc. There is no limit to the humorous skits that can be built off of this concept.

Face Freezing

Participants: 2
Props: None

The following skit usually involves a Scout and a Scoutmaster.

Scout: When you were little did your parents ever tell you that if you made an ugly face for too long, your face might freeze like that?
Scoutmaster: Yes they did.
Scout: Well you can't say you weren't warned.

Sixty Seconds

Participants: 5
Props: None

Five Scouts walk in a line counting quickly:

Scout 1: 1.
Scout 2: 2.
Scout 3: 3.
Scout 4: 4.
Scout 5: 5.
Scout 1: 6.
Scout 2: 7......

The counting continues until Scout 5 reaches the number 60. Then together they all say, "We have just wasted one minute of your time. Thank you."

Pebbles

Participants: 4 to 8
Props: None

The skit begins with the following announcement:

Announcer: Court is in session, the honorable Iwanna B. Fair is presiding.

Judge: You may be seated. Bring in the first plaintiff.

A police officer brings in a plaintiff who is yelling, kicking and screaming...

Plaintiff 1:   I'm innocent, I tell you I was just picking up pebbles on the beach....

Judge to officer: Put him aside and bring in the next plaintiff.

The officer brings in two more plaintiffs with similar stories. The judge handles them in a similar way. The skit ends when the last person is brought on stage. Typically this is a guy dressed like a girl who says in an alluring manner, "Hi, I'm Pebbles."

The Peanut Butter Skit

Participants: 3
Props: Lunch Bag and Peanut Butter Sandwiches

Announcer: *sets the scene.* It is noon, and time for lunch break at a construction site. Here begins Act 1.
Jester: *Takes out lunch, looks into lunch bag, carefully, picks out a sandwich, unwraps it, examines it and scowls.*
Peanut butter!
He then throws sandwich away while others watch.

Announcer: Act 2
Jester: *Takes out lunch, looks into lunch bag, carefully, picks out a sandwich, unwraps it, examines it, scowls and yells* Peanut Butter! *hurls sandwich away while others look on, shaking their heads.*

Announcer: Act 3
Jester: *repeats the actions in act 2 another workman speaks*
Workman: Excuse me for butting in buddy, but I've noticed that every day you look at your sandwich and throw it away. Why don't you tell your wife you don't like Peanut Butter?
Jester: You leave my wife out of this, I make my own sandwiches!

The Tates Compass

Participants: 3 to 4
Props: One or several compasses

The Skitleader hands a compass one at a time to several volunteers or if he has enough compasses, he provides each volunteer with a compass. He then instructs them to find north, being especially careful to keep the compasses clear of their belt buckles. He explains how easy it can be for the compass to point at the metal in the belt rather than at the North Pole. After each successfully finds north or their assigned bearing he congratulates them and says there is one more important thing you must remember. Never use a Tates compass. When one of the participants asks why, the Skitleader replies by saying:

"You know the old saying, he who has a Tates is lost."

Telephone Answering Skit

Participants: 3
Props: None

Three Scouts are needed to perform this skit. They should sit far away from each other, pretending to be speaking on the phone.

Jim: Hello, this is Jim.
Jack: Hello Jim. What's up?
Jim: I'm in Washington and I'm really broke. I need $100 right away. Can you help me out?
Jack: What's that, Jim? I can't hear you. Must be a bad line.
Jim: I'll call you right back.
Ring, Ring
Jack: Hello.
Jim: Jack, it's Jim, I need to borrow $100.
Jack: Jim, I still can't hear what you're saying. We've got a bad connection.
Jim: Let me get the operator to help us. Click. Hello operator can you connect me to Jack.
Jack: Hello.
Jim: Jack, it's me Jim again, I need to borrow $100.
Jack: I still can't hear you.
Operator: Hello, this is the operator. I can hear him clearly.
Jack: Then you give him the $100!

Granny's Candy Store

Participants: 4 performers and 6 volunteers or 7 performers and 3 volunteers
Props: None

The skit begins with the announcer saying how much he used to enjoy going to Granny's candy store. The announcer says that he is going to recreate the scene at Granny's with the help of three performers and six volunteers. One of the performers is assigned the job of being Granny while the other two are told they will be shoppers. Then six volunteers are brought forward, the first three are told to stand in a corner, while the next three are given instructions to play various parts. The first of these plays the part of a cash register (This volunteer stands up and say "Ching, Ching, Ching, repetitively), a popcorn machine, (This volunteer repeats, pop, pop, pop), and a rocking chair, (this volunteer sways back and forth saying, "Creak, Creak, Creak"). The three guys standing in the corner are given no part to play. The shoppers come in and ask Granny for various items, and to each request Granny replies, "I'm sorry dearie, I'm all out of those." Eventually the shoppers get mad and ask, "Well then, what do you have?" Granny answers by stating all she has is these three suckers standing in the corner.

Submarine Training

Participants: 1 plus a volunteer
Props: A cup of water, a picture of a ship, and a raincoat

Storyteller: I need a volunteer to take submarine training. (Put victim under the coat and hold up an arm of the coat to use as a periscope.) Now to be a good submarine captain, you must be able to use the periscope. So let's practice a bit. Can you see the fire? How about those tents? The table? The moon? The stars? (Continues until he becomes proficient.) Let's start our mission. You are the captain of this fine submarine, the SS Tornado. You are to bring it about on maneuvers, and sink enemy ships. So here we go, in the middle of the Atlantic Ocean. Oh! Here comes an enemy ship to the right! Can you see him? (Show a drawing of a ship.) Blow him up! (When he fires, sink the ship.) Good going! Now turn the submarine to port and then to starboard. (Make fun of the volunteer for not knowing port is left & starboard is right) Oh, there's a storm brewing. (Shake him a bit.) Do you see that island? Try to go over there to seek cover. Can you see the waves? My, aren't they big? And they're crashing against the rocks! What a big storm! Can you see it? Can you see the waves? No? (Pour the water down the arm.)

Hardware Store

Participants: 2
Props: None

Scout: (walks in) Have any grapes?
Clerk: No, this is a hardware store.
Scout: (walks in out then back in) Have any grapes?
Clerk: No, this is a hardware store.
Scout: (walks in out then back in) Have any grapes?
Clerk: No! If you ask for grapes one more time, I'll staple your hands to the counter.
Scout: (walks in out then back in) Have any staples?
Clerk: No.
Scout: (laughs) Have any grapes?

Sound in the Wilderness

Participants: 6
Props: None

Participants assume a variety of roles including storyteller, bird, frog, tree, breeze, and Scoutmaster. The Storyteller is telling the story to the campfire crowd, while the other actors, with the exception of the Lost Scoutmaster, have the option to hide in the woods, sit in the crowd, or stand beside the storyteller. The Scoutmaster must hide in the woods.

Storyteller: You know, I love camping. It's not like being in the city at all. You hear sounds that you can only hear out in the country. For example, listen to the chirping of the birds. (Bird chirps a lot, sings a bird song.) Ah, isn't that lovely? And the frogs, they have one of those great sounds. (Frog calls out ribbit sounds.) And though there can be a breeze in the city, it's just not the same as the breeze in the country. (Light breeze being called out.) Let's face it; there are trees in the city, but how many? The breeze through a forest is so nice (Light breeze, slight swishing of the trees.) But the sound I love to hear the most when I go camping is the sound of the Lost Scoutmaster. (Heavy thumping of the feet; calls out, "Where in the world am I?")

The Infantry is Coming

Participants: 2 minimum
Props: Small tree

A Scout runs out on stage yelling, "The infantry is coming, the infantry is coming." Later, (you can do this seconds later or after the next song or skit), a second Scout comes out yelling, "The infantry is coming, the infantry is coming." This happens three or four times. Finally, one or two Scouts come out on stage holding a small tree and they proclaim, "The infant tree is here!"

Pass the Pepper

Participants: 3 or more
Props: Toilet paper, pepper shakers (optional)

Ma: Pass the peppa, Pa.

This message is repeated by each scout in a line up to the last Scout, Pa, who responds:
Pa: Here's the Black Peppa, Ma.

Goes down the line to Ma, who responds:
Ma: No, not the Black Peppa, Pa.

Goes down the line to Pa, who responds:
Pa: Oh. Here's the Chili Peppa, Ma.

This goes on through different kinds of Peppa i.e. Banana Peppa, Jalepeno Peppa, Red Peppa, Green Peppa, and so on until...
Ma: Can't you pass the toilet peppa, Pa?

Don't Brush them on me!

Participants: 2
Props: None

The Scene: A Psychiatrist's office. A patient is laying on the couch. The Doctor is sitting on a chair.

Doctor: Let's see, last week we were talking about your past.
Patient: Yes, I think we were.
Doctor: How much sleep do you get at night?
Patient: Oh, I can't complain. about nine hours I guess.
Doctor: Well, that seems pretty normal. I am beginning to wonder what we are going to find wrong with you. You seem just as sane as I am.
Patient: (horrified) But Doctor, it's these creepy crawly bugs. I just can't stand them! (Leaps from couch and brushes himself wildly). They're all over me, they're all over me.
Doctor: (steps back) Well for goodness sake, don't brush them onto me.

Tag – You're It

Participants: 2
Props: Distinctive clothing, a poncho, a fake mustache, a fake nose and glasses

This skit requires two individuals to dress distinctively so that they are easily recognized later. The first (Scout 1) has a club and is chasing the second (Scout 2) who is running. Scout 2 runs through the audience; he hides behind the master of ceremonies, he climbs a tree, he sits in with the crowd. Scout 2 can be as creative as he desires. Scout 2 must run and Scout 1 must try to grab him. They must both run out of sight without one catching the other.

Later after another skit has been performed, Scout 2 comes into the fire ring panting. He asks, "Has anyone seen Scout 1?" Scout 2 keeps trying to hide, but Scout 1 seems to find him wherever he goes. "Don't tell him where I am," Scout 2 pleads with the audience. Then you hear Scout 1 yelling from beyond the campfire ring, and Scout 2 runs off. Scout 1 chases after him, seemingly intent on blood.

At the next interlude, Scout 1 comes into the fire ring panting and carrying his club. Has anyone seen that no-good Scout 2? Scout 1 is going to get him, and when he catches him he's going to give it to him good. At this point Scout 2 is actually hiding in the audience, wearing a poncho, a fake mustache and glasses. Scout 1 spots him and Scout 2 jumps and runs off.

At the next interlude, the duo comes crashing in again, but Scout 2 trips. Scout 1 towers over him, raises his club, then taps him with his other hand. "You're it!" he intones as he drops the club and runs away. Now Scout 2 picks up the club and chases Scout 1.

Eat that Food

Participants: 3 to 5
Props: A watch, a large quantity of a food item like marshmallows or bananas

This very straightforward skit requires a large quantity of some sort of food item (marshmallows, bananas, bread, prunes or biscuits are good). The skit features a Skitleader and 2 to 4 contestants. The Skitleader announces that we are going to play a game called, "Eat That Food." He selects 2 to 4 contestants from the audience. The contestants are then told that the low bidder will be required to eat 10 marshmallows. Contestants then bet on how long it will take them to eat the ten marshmallows. Whoever bets lowest actually has to do it in that period of time. This skit is based on the Name That Tune game. Actual dialog would go something like this.

Skitleader: to first contestant What is your bid?
1st Contestant: I can eat ten marshmallows in thirty seconds.
2nd Contestant: I can eat that may marshmallows in twenty seconds.
3rd Contestant: I can do it in 5 seconds.
Skitleader: Eat That Food.

20

The Vending Machine

Participants: 2
Props: Pitcher of water, paper cups, quarters

Scout: I'm dying of thirst! Water! Water! What's this? A vending machine?

Vending Mach: DEPOSIT TWENTY-FIVE CENTS PLEASE. The vending machine is a Scout holding a pitcher of water and a cup.

Scout: Twenty-five cents? Oh. Hmm. He takes a quarter out and puts it in the guy's shirt pocket.

Vending Mach: The machine holds out the glass, holds out the pitcher, and mechanically pours the water into the space right next to the glass, missing the glass and pouring on the ground. The Scout desperately tries to grab the water being poured on the ground.

Scout: Water! Water!

Vending Mach: DEPOSIT TWENTY-FIVE CENTS PLEASE. The Scout digs in his pockets, finds another quarter. He puts it in the machine's shirt pocket. The machine holds out the glass, holds out the pitcher, and mechanically pours the water into glass. WATER! The Scout starts to take it, but before he does the machine turns the glass upside down, dumping the water on the ground. The Scout scrambles for the water on the ground, but doesn't get any.

Scout: Water! How do I get water out of this stupid machine?

Vending Mach: DEPOSIT TWENTY-FIVE CENTS PLEASE. The Scout digs in his pockets, finds another quarter. He puts it in the machine's shirt pocket. The machine holds out the glass, holds out the pitcher, and mechanically pours the water into the glass. Then the machine drinks it itself.

Scout: After digging in both pockets I've only got one quarter left. I better get some water this time! The Scout places his last quarter in the machine's pocket, and the machine spits water in his face (the machine stored it in its cheeks when it drank the previous glass)

The Siberian Chicken Farmer

Participants: 4
Props: None

Farmer: Here, chick chick chick … Here, chick chick … chick …
Two military times come up behind the farmer.
Police: Comrade! Vat are you doink?
Farmer: I'm feedink my chickens.
Police: Vat are you feedink dem, Comrade?
Farmer: Corn.
Police: Fool! There is a shortage of corn!!!
They beat him up. Oof. Ow.
Police: *dragging him away* Three years in the work camps for you!
Narrator: Three years later, …
Farmer: Here, chick chick chick … Here, chick chick … chick …
Two military times come up behind the farmer.
Farmer: *stands up* Uh oh …
Police: Comrade! Vat are you doink?
Farmer: I'm feedink my chickens.
Police: Vat are you feedink dem, Comrade?
Farmer: Wheat.
Police: Fool! There is a shortage of wheat!!!
They beat him up. Oof. Ow.
Police: *dragging him away* Five years in the work camps for you!
Narrator: Five years later, …
Farmer: Here, chick chick chick … Here, chick chick … chick …
Two military times come up behind the farmer.
Farmer: *stands up* Uh oh.
Police: Comrade! Vat are you doink?
Farmer: I'm feedink my chickens.
Police: Vat are you feedink them, Comrade?
Farmer: Rubles.
Police: Rubles? But vy are you feedink them rubles, Comrade?
Farmer: They can buy their own food!

The Echo (American Style)

Participants: 2
Props: None

The skit leader announces during the singing that he has noticed an echo around the campfire and he is going to demonstrate how the echo works. The following dialogue takes place between the leader and the echo (a skit performer who is out of site).

Leader: Hello.
Echo: Hello.
Leader: Bread.
Echo: Bread.
Leader: Cheese.
Echo: Cheese.
Leader: Baloney.
Echo: (silence)
Leader: Baloney.
Echo: (silence)
Leader: (acting surprised and embarrassed) The echo must have stopped working. Let me try again. (He then says in a louder voice) This leader is great.
Echo: Baloney.

The Echo (British Style)

Participants: 2
Props: None

One participant, "The Echo," hides in the woods behind the campfire while the other, "The Scout," comes to the front of the campfire.

Scout: Boy, it's been a tough day at camp. But now I've hiked up to the famous Echo Mountain, might as well give it a try. (raises voice) Testing …1…2… 3…
Echo: Testing.
Scout: I'm a Boy Scout and I'm trained to live in the woods, (raises voice) right!
Echo: Right.

Scout: And when it's my turn to cook, if I mess up the stew the rest of the guys can lump it, *(raises voice)* correct!
Echo: Correct!
Scout: And I'll tell that to the Scoutmaster too. *(raises voice)* Check!
Echo: Check!
Scout: *turning to hike away, in an arrogant tone* No one's gonna push me around and treat me like a JERK.
Echo: JERK! *Scout does a double take and exits.*

The Dead Body

Participants: 3
Props: None

A Scout is lying on the ground pretending to be dead. Another walks up and finds the "Dead" Scout lying on the ground. A third Scout is off in the distance, acting as a police dispatcher receiving a call.

Scout 2: Hello, hello, is this the police?
Scout 3: Yes, it is.
Scout 2: I've just found a dead body at the corner of Sycamore and First Avenue.
Scout 3: Can you spell that?
Scout 2: Uh, S I K (looking around for a sign), no I mean S Y K.....wait a minute, let me drag him over to First and Elm.

The Announcement

Participants: 2
Props: None

MC: And now it's time to make a spot announcement.
Second Scout: Makes the sound of a dog barking.
MC: Thank you Spot.

The Lighthouse

Participants: 7 to 11
Props: 1 or 2 flashlights

This skit requires a narrator, 3 to 5 Scouts and an equal number of Scout leaders. Scouts play the role of lighthouse walls. Leaders will be "recruited" from the audience to assume a "support position." The skit begins with scouts standing in a circle, facing out, with their feet touching, (their feet are spread 2 – 3' apart). A single flashlight (or optionally 2 if more than four Scouts are used), is held at eye level and is passed around the circle. Scouts stand tall and hold the beacon's beam steady. The Narrator begins:

Narrator: Many years ago the people of a seaside village built a lighthouse to warn approaching ships of a dangerous shoal near their harbor. The beacon from this lighthouse could be seen for miles, even in fog and storms. For many decades, the lighthouse stood firm and gave safe passage to all who sailed by the village. But as the years went by, the villagers grew old and so did the lighthouse. The villagers could no longer make repairs, the ocean's waves wore away the foundation. The weary lighthouse sagged and failed in its duty.

The Scouts now bend at the waist, with their heads leaning toward the side. They bend their knees slightly and pass the light around, shining it erratically.

Narrator: When the schooners and square riggers started to go aground on the shoals, the old villagers knew they had to call in experienced people to help solve their problem. People who were pillars in their own communities and who were as solid as rock. They turned to the leadership of The Boy Scouts of America.

The Narrator now calls on some of the prestigious area leadership and instructs them to come forth and support their falling lighthouse. He instructs them to go down on their hands and knees and into holes in the walls (between the scouts' legs). Leaders are facing in with their derrieres out, and are straddled by the Scouts who again stand tall and give a steady light.

Narrator: Now with these new rocks placed into the foundation, the lighthouse once again shines a bright beacon and stands firm in the stormy surf to withstand the pounding of the waves.

Scouts drop the flashlight and then hand paddle the leaders.

Be Prepared

Participants: 2
Props: None

Scout 1:   What's the difference between a Scout and a guy who fixes telephone answering machines?
Scout 2:   The Scout's motto is "Be Prepared" and the other guy's motto is "Beep Repaired!"

Morning Coffee

Participants: 2
Props: None

Scoutmaster: *to Scout* This coffee tastes like mud!
Scout: That's funny; it was just ground this morning.

I'm Leaving

Participants: 2
Props: Garbage bag, leaves

The first Scout walks across the area scattering handfuls of leaves he takes from a big bag. Another Scout approaches and asks, "What are you doing?"
The first Scout replies, "I'm leaving!"

The Complaining Monk

Participants: 3
Props: None

Narrator: This skit is about the monks in a monastery who are only allowed to speak two words every ten years. Our friendly monk is about to come in and say his two words, after ten long years of silence.

Abbot: *(Chants some blessing, then,)* Yes, my son, what do you wish to say?

Monk: Bad food!

Narrator: Well, ten years have gone by, and of course our friendly monk's time has come again to say his two words. He of course is not quite as young as he used to be, and walks a touch more slowly.

Abbot: *(Chants some blessing, then,)* Yes, my son, what do you wish to say?

Monk: Uncomfortable bed!

Narrator: Well, yet another ten years have gone by, and of course our friendly monk's time has come again to say his two words. He is really old at this point, having been at the monastery for thirty, long, devoted years.

Abbot: *(Chants some blessing, then,)* Yes, my son, what do you wish to say?

Monk: I quit!

Abbot: I'm not surprised! You've been here for thirty years and all you've done is complain!

Three Scouts

Participants: 6 to 9
Props: None

Three Scouts, an Eagle, First Class and a Tenderfoot, are running from the police and a group of bloodhounds. They reach the point of exhaustion and are about to get caught, so they climb some trees. Three Scouts already positioned in trees can assume the roles of the Eagle, First Class, and Tenderfoot Scout, or the original three can simply hide behind trees while the announcer explains these three Scouts have climbed the trees.

The dogs go to the first tree, with the police officers right behinds them. The Eagle Scout does bird imitations in an attempt to fool the dogs. A police officer retorts, "Dumb dogs, there's nothing but birds up that tree!"

The group goes to the next tree where the First Class Scout does a cat imitation. "Dumb dogs, that's just a cat!"

Finally they go to the third tree, where the Tenderfoot is hiding. The Tenderfoot begins shouting, "Moooo, Mooo, Moooo!"

Variations:
Alternatively the Eagle Scout can be assigned the role of the goat. An announcer can be used to set the stage for this skit. An unlimited amount of Scouts can optionally be employed in this skit to play the part of police officers and dogs.

The Bucket Fisherman

Participants: 2
Props: Bucket, pole, and string

A Scout sits at the front of the campfire holding a fishing pole. The end of the fishing line is sitting in a bucket as if the Scout is fishing in the bucket. The Scout begins to pull on the line as if he has just hooked a large fish. At this moment a second Scout walks past the fisherman, does a double-take and walks over to talk to the fisherman. They begin a dialogue that can go something like this:

Passerby: Hey, Joe what are you doing?
Fisherman: I'm fishing, silly, what does it look like I'm doing?
Passerby: Fishing? What are you fishing for?
Fisherman: I'm fishing for suckers.
Passerby: Have you caught any?
Fisherman: Yes, as a matter of fact, you're the third today.

Gold Appraiser

Participants: 4
Props: Bags filled with rocks or candy, a table

The skit begins with a gold appraiser sitting behind a table. Prospectors come in with their gold and ask the appraiser to value it.

Scout 1: (Walks in with a bag of rocks) Can you tell me what this is and how much it's worth?
Appraiser: It's Fool's Gold and it worthless.
Scout 1: What'll I do with it?
Appraiser: Leave it hear, I'll take care of it.
Scout 2: (Walks in with a bag of rocks or candy and repeats the action)
Can you tell me what this is?
Appraiser: It's Fool's Gold and it worthless.
Scout 1: What'll I do with it?
Appraiser: Leave it hear, I'll take care of it.
Scout 3: (A third miner walks in) What do you have there?
Appraiser: I got dem fools' gold!

The King's Raisins

Participants: 4 to 7
Props: None

King: I am the King. Bring me my raisins!
1st Squire: Here are raisins, sire, from the hills of California!
King: Those raisins are not fit for peasants! Bring me my raisins!
2nd Squire: Here are raisins, sire, from the vineyards of France!
King: They are hardly worth sneezing at. Bring me my raisins!
3rd Squire: These raisins, sire, were handpicked with tweezers by Benedictine Monks in Germany!
King: These raisins are NO GOOD! Bring me my royal raisin supplier!
Two squires drag in the royal raisin supplier.
King: Why have you not brought me my raisins?
Royal Supplier: My rabbit died!

The Bee Sting

Participants: 2
Props: None

Scout 1: OOOOOOUCH, OOOOOH, OOOUCH!
Scout 2: What's the matter?
Scout 1: A bee stung my thumb.
Scout 2: Try putting some ointment on it.
Scout 1: But the bee will be miles away by now.

The Cancer Sketch

Participants: 4
Props: Tin can (A knife, fork, salt & pepper shaker, tweezers and wrench are optional.)

Three scouts surround a scout lying down.
Scout 1: Doctor, do you think you can save him?
Doctor: I don't know. The patient has a bad case of cancer. This will be tough. Knife.
The assistant hands the doctor a knife.
Assistant: Knife, sir.
The doctor sticks out his hand.
Doctor: Fork.
The assistant hands him a fork.
Assistant: Fork, sir.
Doctor: Salt and Pepper.
The assistant hands him salt and pepper.
Assistant: Salt and pepper, sir.
Doctor: I have found the liver. Monkey wrench.
The assistant hands the doctor a monkey wrench.
Doctor: I have found the cancer. Tweezers, there, that should do it.
Assistant: You have removed the can, sir!
The assistant holds up an old tin can.

The Rabbit Skit

Participants: 2
Props: None

Scout 1: Ask me if I'm a rabbit.
Scout 2: Okay Are you a rabbit?
Scout 1: Yes. Now ask me if I'm a beaver.
Scout 2: Are you a beaver?
Scout 1: No, silly. I already told you I was a rabbit!

The Blanket Tossing Team

Participants: 5 to 7
Props: A blanket (optional)

This takes about six guys, who form a circle around an invisible blanket, with a small invisible guy (Hector) who sits in the middle of the invisible blanket and gets tossed.

We're an Olympic blanket tossing team, and Hector in the middle here is our star blanket bouncer. We'll toss Hector a bit just to warm up. One, two, three! One, two, three! One, two, three!

On three each time, the team lets the pretend blanket go slack, then pull it taut. They watch the invisible Hector go up in the air, then come down, and they gently catch him again in the blanket. Each time they toss him higher. The team has to be in sync, and they have to watch about the same spot -- the easiest way to do this is to have everyone just imitate the leader, who is the speaker.

OK, we're all limbered up now? The team murmurs in agreement. Then let's toss Hector a bit higher. One, two, three!

Hector comes up, and the team adjusts their position a bit to catch him as he comes down.
One, two, three! This time wait about ten seconds, and move quite a bit to get under him. Move this way and that before finally catching him.

One, two, three! Twenty seconds this time, almost lose track of him, adjust the position here, there, and here again.

What? What's that you say, Hector? pause Audience, you are in luck! Hector wants to go for the world record blanket toss! Ready team? One! Two! Thrreee!!! A mighty toss! The team shifts positions, like trying to catch a high fly ball. There he goes! He's past the trees! He's really up there! *pause, looking hard into the sky* Do you see him? I've lost him. Where'd he go? *another pause* Oh well. *The team leaves the stage, and the program continues.*

After another skit and song, and preferably in the middle of awards or announcements of some sort, Hector! Quick team! *The blanket tossing team runs back on stage, positions themselves this way and that, and catches Hector.* Let's have a big hand for Hector! Hurrah!!!

Future Astronauts

Participants: 3 minimum.
Props: None

Setting: Three Scouts are bragging about their futures as astronauts.

1st Scout: When I grow up, I'm going to Mars.
2nd Scout: Well, I'm going to Neptune.
3rd Scout: I'm going to the Sun.

(1st two Scouts scoff at this last statement.)

1st Scout: It's too hot on the sun.
2nd Scout: Yeah, your rocket will melt.
3rd Scout: What do you think I am? Stupid? I'm going at night!

It's All Around Me

Participants: 2
Props: Belt

A Scout runs into the room yelling, "It's all around me! It's all around me!" A second Scout asks, "What's around you?" The first Scout replies, "My belt."

If I Were Not a Boy Scout

Participants: 4 to 8
Props: none

This is a very popular skit. There are many verses and it can be fun to make up your own. This skit is unique in many respects; first this skit is sung; secondly, it is acted out. Individuals are assigned a part to sing and actions that go with their part. It is also unique in that the skit is progressive. It begins with one participant singing and acting out his part and ends when the last participant is part of the action. Finally, this skit is cumulative. Each new person comes in and performs their line; then everyone does their lines at the same time.

The skit begins with 4 to 8 participants standing in a line at the front of the campfire singing the chorus as a group:

The Chorus is sung to the following tune:

Refrain:
g c   c   d d e   c
If I were not a Boy Scout,
g c   c   d d   e
I know what I would be,
g c c   d d e   c
If I were not a Boy Scout,
g c   c   d d   e (hold this last note)
I know what I would be....

The first person takes one step forward and says...
A Garbage Man I'd be.
He stands there while the rest of the group sings...
If he were not a Boy Scout, a Garbage Man he'd be....
Then "garbage man" says:
Lift it, dump it, pull out the Goodies.
The "garbage man" acts out each of these operations (what he sings) with hand and body motions.
Lift it, dump it, pull out the Goodies.
The "garbage man" steps back into line and the Chorus is sung again. After the Chorus is sung (2 times) the next person in line steps forward.
A Chicken Plucker I'd be.
He stands out front while the line sings.

If he were not a Boy Scout, a Chicken Plucker he would be…..
Then the Chicken Plucker sings…
Pluck a chicken, pluck a chicken, ring its little neck.
(appropriate and exaggerated, hand motions that match his words)
Pluck a chicken, pluck a chicken, ring its little neck.

NOW starts the fun … after the newest singer does his part twice, he does it 2 more times and is accompanied by the first singer ("The Garbage Man") singing his part twice. It will be difficult to hear the words with both singing at once but the actions will tell the story. This continues building through all of the "characters", ending with "If we were not a Boy Scout, this is what we'd be" sung fairly slowly while going to a lower note each time, all 8, or 10 arms out in a dramatic Al Jolson/Broadway show finish.

Additional Characters:
Fireman: Jump baby, jump, ooooooo – splat.
Ice Cream Man: Tooty fruity, tooty, fruity, nice ice cream *(usually done effeminately)*
Cyclist: Peddle peddle, peddle peddle, ring-ring-ring *(also can be done effeminately)*
Carpenter: Two by four, nail it to the floor! Owww!
Farmer: Come on Bessie give, the baby's got to live! Ugh!
Birdwatcher: Hark! A lark! Flying through the park! Splat!
Plumber: Plunge it, flush it, look out below!
Surgeon: Cut'em, stitch'em, oops where does this go?
Computer programmer: Push the button, push the button, kick the damn machine.
Slot machine: Pull the handle, pull the handle, put a nickel in.
Ballerina: Tippy-toe, tippy-toe, do a pirouette.
Hippie: Ooh man, cool man, far out wow!
Hippie:(Alternate) Love, peace, my hair is full of grease.
Lumberjack: Chip-chop, chip-chop, oh no!
Scoutmaster: Do this, do that, don't do that.
Scoutmaster: (Alternate) Do this, do that, I'm gonna take a nap
Farmer: (Alternate) There-a-cow (point), there-a-cow (point), eeee-yyy-uuu-kkk (foot in cow patty).
Police Officer: Sllrrrpp – ahhhh (from a cup of coffee) License and registration please!
Bill & Ted: (two people) Excellent (point). Bogus (point).

Evangelist: Well-well, you never can tell. You might go to Heaven, and you might go to Hell!
Teenage Father: I swear, I swear, I wasn't even there!
Airline steward: Coffee, airsick bag, BBLLLAAARRCCHH!

Alternative Verses:

This skit has been adapted and changed many times. Some popular variations include:

If I were not a Buffalo…
If I were not a Scoutmaster…
If I were not a Camper…
If we were not Boy Scouts here's what we be…

Campfire Conference

Participants: 6 to 8
Props: none

Six or eight weary-looking campers enter the campfire circle, silently circling the campfire once, and then sitting in a ring around the fire. After a long pause, the first camper sighs and says, "What a day!" There's another pause for deliberation before the second camper sighs and says, "What a day!", and yet another before the third repeats, and so on around the circle until they reach the last camper. He sighs and says, "You betcha." The first camper then turns and says in disgust, "If you can't stick to the subject, I'm getting out of here!" Then he rises and leaves the campfire, followed by all the others.

The Commercial

Participants: 3 or more
Props: None

Director: Okay, people! Let's get going!
Cameraman: But sir!
Director: No interruptions! Action!

Actor:	(speaking in overly dull voice), Drink Scout Splash. It tastes great and is made from the best stuff on earth, stuff like used dishwater, beaver sweat.....''(The Director interrupts)
Director:	Cut! That sounded like you don't like the stuff! Sound sincere! Okay! Let's try it again!
Cameraman:	But sir!
Director:	No buts! Action!

(The Actor begins again this time with the appropriate level of sincerity. The interruptions by the director and cameraman continue, with the director saying things like it's too fast, too slow, whispers into the actor's ear (who then checks his zipper) until finally, everything goes smoothly. While the Cameraman keeps on saying but sir, or there is something I need to tell you, with the director cutting the cameraman off each time)

Director:	Cut! And print! That was fantastic! Let's get out of here!
Cameraman:	But sir! We don't have any film!

Optionally, the director can chase the cameraman off.

You Don't Say

Participants: 2
Props: Phone

Scout 1: (pretends to answer a phone) Hello? Yes? You don't say ... You don't say ... You don't say ... You don't say? ... You don't say! ... You don't say. Bye!
Scout 2: Say, who was on the phone?
Scout 1: He didn't say!

Magic Chair

Participants: 5
Props: Two Chairs

Scene begins with doctor sitting on one of the chairs. The first patient enters twitching their left arm.

Doctor: And what's wrong with you?
Patient 1: As you can see doctor I have this terrible twitch.
Doctor: Just sit on my magic chair and you'll get better.
The patient sits on the chair and stops twitching, but the doctor's left arm starts twitching.
Patient 1: Oh thank you doctor. you cured me.
The patient leaves, the doctor still twitching calls for the next patient.
Doctor: Next......And what's wrong with you?
This patient has the hiccups. The process of sitting in the chair is repeated. The doctor now has a twitch and the hiccups. The third patient is called in, both his legs keep flicking in the air. The process is again repeated so that the doctor now has a twitching arm the hiccups and both legs flicking in the air. The doctor now calls patient four. This patient looks quite normal, enters and sits in the magic chair.
Doctor: And what may I ask is wrong with you sir?
Patient 4: I've got a terrible case of the runs doc.
The doctor runs off the stage holding his stomach.

The Human Xylophone

Participants: 5 or more
Props: None

The skit is performed by a Skitleader who states that he is going to play a song on a human xylophone. Several boys kneel in a line at the front of the campfire. Each is assigned the part of a musical note. They are told to speak or hum a musical key whenever they are touched on the head. They can all say the word "La" or each can be assigned a different word like "do, re, mi, fa, so, la, ti,). Simple songs such as "Twinkle, Twinkle Little Star," can be played out this way. With practice, harder songs like, "Scout Vespers," can be played. Regardless of the song performed, this skit requires thorough practice.

Variation 1: A conductor can be added to lead this team. Scouts can be instructed to sing their note in a higher or lower pitch based on how high or low the conductor raised his hand. The conductor can provide additional comedy t this sketch by raising his arm higher and higher or by placing his hand near the ground for Scouts to try and hit impossibly low notes. Optionally, the conductor can cover his ears, or turn away from performers who sing off key.

Emergency Broadcast System

Participants: 4 to 10
Props: None

A group of Scouts gather in front of the audience. On queue everyone in the group hums in a high pitched tone, very similar to what you might hear on the radio during an emergency broadcast system alert. After a about 20 seconds the humming stops and an MC or Scout from the group comes forward and says, "This has been a test of the Camp/Pack/Troop _____ Emergency Broadcast System. This was only a test. If this had been an actual emergency, what you would hear would sound like this." Immediately following this speech all the Scouts in the group begin screaming and running in all different directions in what appears to be a terrified panic.

The Viper

Participants: 3 or more
Props: (optional) Squeegee and sponge or toilet paper

This skit has many variations. Here's two....

An Assistant Patrol Leader runs to the front of the campfire and informs the Patrol Leader that he has just received a message that the Viper is coming. The Patrol Leader gets very agitated and upset repeating the Assistant's message. Several others come in repeating the same message. They are all in a state of panic when the last person comes on stage with a squeegee and a sponge announcing, "I'm the vindov viper. I've come to vipe your vindovs. Vhere do I start?"

Variation

Four Scouts run out in succession. The first says something like "here comes the viper, hide". Scouts 2, 3 and 4 make similar comments. The final Scout ends the skit with the following punch-line, "Hi I'm the viper. (optionally holding out the roll of toilet paper) Does anyone need viping?"

The Crying Skit

Participants: 4 to 5
Props: Handkerchiefs

A Scout comes on stage crying. A second Scout comes out and asks the first Scout what's wrong. The first Scout whispers in the second Scout's ear and they both start crying, long and loud. Several others come out one at a time, and repeat the same action. When everyone is on stage, crying, moaning, howling, sniffing and so on (using large handkerchiefs that were dipped in water before their entrance and wringing them out splashily,) the last participant comes out and asks aloud: "Why is everyone crying?" They all answer in unison: "Because we haven't got a skit!"

Forty-Nine

Participants: 2
Props: Garbage can lid or cardboard cut-out to simulate a man-hole cover

A person is jumping on up and down, yelling 49! 49! 49! The second person comes by and notices this; he asks what he is doing.

Victim: What are you doing?
Jumper: I'm jumping up and down on this manhole yelling 49! 49! 49! It's really fun! Wanna try?
Victim: Sure!

He takes the jumper's place and yells 49! 49! 49! All of a sudden, the jumper pulls the manhole cover out from under the victim, who pretends to fall into the sewer. The jumper replaces the lid and begins again....

Jumper: 50! 50! 50!

Multiple Births

Participants: 4 or 5
Props: None

One Scout plays the part of a doctor. The other three play dads sitting in a hospital waiting room. Optionally an announcer can set the scene.

Doctor: Mr. Jones, congratulations. You're the proud father of twins!
Jones: What a coincidence-I come from Two Mountains!
Later...
Doctor: Mr. Smith, you now have triplets!
Smith: That's quite astonishing! I come from Three Rivers!
Third father faints; doctor revives him.
Doctor: Mr. Smart-what's wrong? Your wife hasn't even given birth yet!
Smart: I come from Thousand Islands!

The Poison Spring

Participants: 4 or more
Props: 2 or 3 ladles, 1 bucket, rice or confetti

One by one the participants drag themselves on stage crying for water. Each reaches a bucket with a ladle and takes a drink, splashing some water to show there is really water in it and dies. Generally, boys get a good audience reaction by "hamming up" the death scene. More than a ladle will probably be needed so that there is plenty of water to slosh around. The next to the last person starts to drink from the bucket, when the final Scout comes in. Seeing all the dead bodies, the last Scout yells, "Don't drink from that bucket, the water has been poisoned." Then the last Scout runs on stage, grabs the bucket and throws it on the audience. Of course, other than the water that was in the ladles the bucket is empty or contains something harmless like rice or confetti.

Scientific Genius

Participants: 3 or more
Props: Rocket ship (cardboard cutout)

The announcer tells the audience they are at the scene of a secret governmental test site where a highly classified rocket is to be launched by America's leading scientists. A rocket and or launching pad cut out of cardboard can be used as a prop in this skit. After an elaborate countdown, the rocket fails to launch at zero. After unexpected gasps and questions about what could possibly have gone wrong, those present inspect it. Using highly scientific sounding terms, the participants examine a number of highly scientific sounding devices - the supersonic sector compressor; the thermonuclear 0-rings, the triamedic rocket fuel igniters, etc. All seem perfect. Finally, a young Scout walks out of the audience and says, "I think I see the problem. Someone forgot to put fuel in the rocket.... "

The Shrimpy Boxer

Participants: 3
Props: Frying pan

Generally an older larger Scout performs this skit with a Cub Scout or younger Scout.

Version 1
Announcer: *(loudly)* Ladies and Gentlemen. May I bring your attention to the center ring where we will have our main attraction! Little John will be fighting against a new contender, named Shrimpy! 1-2-3 Go!

The fight begins. As they box Shrimpy gets hit left and right. He is losing big until at the last moment, he throws one weak punch and Little John falls unconscious.

Announcer: 1! 2! 3! Shrimpy wins! Now let's look at that in slow motion!

Boxers get up, and the scene repeats itself slowly in slow motion. When Shrimpy is throwing his punch, someone quickly (someone operating at high speed while the other remains in slow motion), runs up and swings the frying pan against Little John's head.

Version 2

Another version of this skit operates in a manner similar to version 1 except that the fight never begins. As the announcer is explaining the rules, he demonstrates various forbidden behaviors (you may have seen Elmer Fudd and Daffy Duck perform this gag). The announcer says, "We'll have none of this!" *(kicks Little John in the groin)* "Or this!" *(breaks arm over his knee)* "Or this!" *(kicks in the knees)* "And of course this is prohibited!" *(hits over the head with the frying pan)* "Understood? Good! Go!"

Of course by this point Little John is so woozy that one weak punch from Shrimpy knocks him out.

The Lost Quarter

Participants: 5 minimum
Props: Sleeping bags.

Scene: One person acts as a lamppost, shining a flashlight on the ground. Another is groping around in the pool of light. (He's Camper 1). Camper 3 enters, sees Scout 1, and begins the dialog:

Camper 3:   What are you looking for?
Camper 1:   A quarter that I lost.

Camper 3 joins Camper 1, and helps him search. Other Campers enter and repeat the above scene. Finally the last scout to enter turns to Camper 1 and asks:

Last Camper: Where did you lose the quarter?
Camper 1:   (Pointing away) Over there.
Last Camper: Then why are you looking here?"
Camper 1:   Because the light is better over here!

The Royal Message

Participants: 5
Props: Pots and pans

King: Listen carefully everyone! The palace is surrounded by enemy warriors the knights of the Yellow Fingers. I must get a message through to my friend, the King of Sardinia, so that he can send his army to assist us. Sir Lancelot, take this message [hands note] and go as fast as you can.

Lancelot: Yes, your Majesty. [Lancelot exits. Off-stage Lancelot yells and groans, while pots and pans are banged by offstage assistants to simulate a battle. Lancelot reenters limping.]

Lancelot: They're a vicious band your Majesty. I could not fight my way through!

King: Off to the hospital with you. Sir Ramsbottom, take this message and go forth.

Ramsbottom: I'll do my best your Kingship. [Ramsbottom exits. Off-stage Ramsbottom yells and groans, while pots and pans are banged by offstage assistants to simulate a battle Ramsbottom reenters limping. His arm hangs limply].

Ramsbottom: I fought like a wild man your Kingship, but it is was no use.

King: Go and join Lancelot in the hospital. Sir Farthingsworth, it is your turn. The Kingdom depends on you!

Farthingsworth: Yes my Liege. I'll get the message through! [Actions are performed as before].

Farthingsworth: [returns crawling in] There is no hope my Liege.

King: Off you go to join the others. Pages, come here! You have seen how terrible this gang is, but I have no choice. You must take the message.

Pages: [in unison] Gladly your Majesty. [exit skipping]

King: [pacing around campfire] Probably all is lost. They have been gone a long time now, but I heard no sounds of battle. They probably killed the little fellows off just like that. [snaps fingers]

Pages: *[enter skipping]* There you are your Majesty, a return message from the King of Sardinia.

King: You've done it! You've done it! However did you manage?

Pages: *[breaking into song]* Let your Pages do the walking though the Yellow Fingers.

The Making of a Great Bonfire

Participants: 3 skitleaders and many volunteers
Props: None

This skit should be reserved for a warm summer evening. A scoutleader and two or more assistants stand at the front of the campfire. The Scoutleader begins a dialog that contains instructions for the assistants and can go something like this:

Scoutleader: Many people have asked how we managed to build such a nice bonfire. As our Scout skills discussion for this evening, I am going to demonstrate the technique behind building a crisscross lay bonfire. My assistants will begin by collecting firewood. They begin by gathering kindling.

The assistants select various members of the audience to represent different pieces of wood. Some smaller Scouts are bunched in the middle to represent kindling, while larger Scouts and leaders are selected to be logs. These logs are then stacked on top of each other. The Scoutleader continues issuing instructions to his assistants while describing the process of making a fire. The monologue ends with a dialog that can go something like this.

Scoutleader: ....the fire is then ready to start. When creating a bonfire, perhaps the most important thing to remember is safety. When the fire is over make sure the fire is good and out as demonstrated here by my faithful assistants. The assistants then come forward with buckets and throw water on the volunteers that represent the make-believe fire.

Animal Impressions

Participants: 3 or 4
Props: None

The announcer selects volunteers who come forward. These volunteers are told they can win prizes if they can get an audience member to successfully guess what animal sound or call they have been instructed to make. The announcer then whispers in the volunteer's ear, or alternatively hands the volunteer a piece of paper, indicating what animal call the volunteer is to make. Early volunteers are given animals that are easy to imitate, like a cow (the volunteer says "moo"), horse ("neigh"), or sheep ("baa"). Each volunteer is heartily congratulated on a job well done as the audience successfully identifies their animal call; these volunteers are then awarded prizes (real or imaginary). The final volunteer ("the victim") is then selected. Try to choose an adult leader or an older Scout with a good sense of humor. This volunteer is told to make the call of some animals that the audience will not be able to guess. This can be animals that no one has ever heard of like the fissiroal bill goatsucker, muskox, anfrican jerboa, pangolin (an asian anteater), wombat, etc. or you can choose animals that make little or no sound like rabbits, deer, or skunks. As the audience is unable to identify each animal the announcer says, "Oh, I'm sorry the audience just can't seem to identify your impression. Let's give our volunteer another try." The volunteer is then given the name of another animal that is impossible to imitate.

There are various options that can be used to end this skit. Generally the skit ends after the audience is unable to guess the victim's third animal impression. This can simply be an impossible animal to impersonate or it can be a Wild Boar, Old Goat, or Jackass. The skit then ends when the announcer says, "For those of you who were unable to guess, our volunteer is a …..(Wild Boar, Old Goat, or Jackass)."

Nosebleed

Participants: 4 or 5
Props: None

The first Scout (Nosebleed person) is looking down at the ground.
Scout 2 comes in and looks around, then down, and mumbles:
Scout 2:   Hmm, what's going down, man? (No answer.)
Scout 3 walks in, does the same thing, as does 4
Scout 5:   *Walks in, looks up for a moment, and then speaks:*
         What are you guys doing?
Nosebleed: I don't know what these guys are doing, but I've got a nosebleed!

The Uniform Shop

Participants: 4 or 5
Props: Scout Uniform

Shopkeeper: Hello everyone, welcome to my store.
Shopper 1:   Hi, I'd like to buy a Scout shirt.
Storekeeper: Sure. One moment, please.
The sound of a kid struggling with the shopkeeper is heard in the background. The kid in the background speaks...
Kid: No, you can't have it!
The Shop keeper comes back with a shirt to a Scout uniform.
Shopper 2:   I'd like to buy the accessories to the Scout uniform.
Shopkeeper: Sure. One moment, please.
You hear the kid struggling with the keeper in the background-"No, you can't have them!" Then the Shopkeeper comes back with accessories.
Shopper 3:   I'd like to buy the pants to go with the Scout uniform.
Shopkeeper: Sure. One moment, please.
You hear the kid struggling with the keeper in the background-"No, you can't have them." Then the Shopkeeper comes back with pants.
Shopper 4:   I'd like to buy the right kind of shoes for the Scout uniform.
Shopkeeper: Sure. One moment, please.
You hear the kid struggling with the keeper in the background, "No, you can't have them!" The Shopkeeper then comes back with shoes. Finally the kid comes running out in underwear/swim suit.
Kid: How am I supposed to go to Scouts without my uniform?

The Factory Guard

Participants: 4 or 5
Props: Empty cardboard boxes

Manager: (To new guard) I'm giving you the very responsible position of gate guard at this factory. Because of the lack of vigilance by your predecessors, the workers have stolen so many finished articles that the firm is heading for bankruptcy. Your duty is to ensure this is brought to an end. Do you understand?

Guard: Yes, sir. I am to stop stealing.

Manager: That's right. You can search people if necessary. Now it's up to you, and let's see some results.

Guard: Very good, Sir.

Manager leaves; guard takes post; first workman enters carrying a box with a blanket draped over it.

Guard: Just a moment. What have you got in that box?

Employee 1: What do you mean?

Guard: What have you got in that box? It's my duty to see that no one takes stuff out of the factory.

Employee 1: Why didn't you say? There's nothing in the box. Look!

He shows everyone the box is empty.

Guard: Oh, well, that's all right then.

#1 leaves and #2 enters, box draped as before. Guard and workman go through routine of looking in the box. Repeat with #3. After #3 has left, the manager races in enraged.

Manager: What's the matter with you? I hired you to stop this pilfering. You've only been here half an hour and already we're losing things!

Guard: But the only people who went out were three men with boxes. I stopped them all and they all had nothing in them.

Manager: We make boxes!

Order your Scout Fun Books today!

Scout Riddles

Superior Campfires

The Scout Puzzle & Activity Book

Scout Skits

Scout Jokes

Scoutmaster's Minutes

Scoutmaster's Minutes II

More Scout Skits

Along the Scouting Trail

Campfire Tales

Run-ons and Even More Scout Skits

Scout Games

For an updated list of available books along with current pricing visit: *scoutfunbooks.webs.com*
or find our books on Amazon!

Books are also available on a wholesale basis to qualified Scout Troops, Council Shops, trading posts in quantities of 50 or more. Contact us by email at BoyScoutBooks@aol.com.

Made in America

22995004R00028

Made in the USA
Columbia, SC
01 August 2018